MW01134143

To Forest and Fig, with mountains of love.
—A. H.

To my Matt, who has always been—and ever will be—my big rock.
—N. L.

Library of Congress Cataloging-in-Publication Data:

Names: Huntington, Amy, author. | Lemon, Nancy, illustrator.
Title: How to make a mountain / by Amy Huntington ; illustrated by
    Nancy Lemon.
Description: San Francisco, California : Chronicle Kids, [2022] |
    Audience: Ages 5-8. | Audience: K to grade 3. | Summary: "Geology
    and earth science made easy (to learn) and super-quick (to read
    about). You, too, can make a mountain—start today! (Some
    restrictions apply.)"— Provided by publisher.
Identifiers: LCCN 2019012176 | ISBN 9781452175881 (alk. paper)
Subjects: LCSH: Mountains—Juvenile literature. | Mountain biodiversity—
    Juvenile literature. | Orogeny—Juvenile literature.
Classification: LCC GB512 .H86 2022 | DDC 551.8/2--dc23
LC record available at https://lccn.loc.gov/2019012176

Manufactured in China.

Design by Alice Seiler.
Typeset in Mark and Mr Dodo.
The illustrations in this book were rendered digitally and in pencil and gouache.

10 9 8 7 6 5 4 3 2 1

Chronicle Books LLC
680 Second Street
San Francisco, California 94107

Chronicle Books—we see things differently.
Become part of our community at www.chroniclekids.com.

HOW TO MAKE A
MOUNTAIN

in Just 9 Simple Steps and Only 100 Million Years!

By
Amy Huntington

Illustrated by
Nancy Lemon

chronicle books
san francisco

Let's make a mountain,

a big one with steep cliffs, boulders, streams, and waterfalls. Tiny plants and towering trees full of birdsong. Wandering raccoons, porcupines, bears, and deer.

Of course, you will want a rocky, windswept summit for a bird's-eye view.

It's going to take a little muscle and a whole lot of patience. It *is* a big job, but it's packed with adventure.

Load up your gear, and get ready for the challenge of a lifetime!

STEP 1:

FIND A ROCK

Making a mountain takes
millions and millions of years.

But all you really need to start is a big rock.

← THINK SUPER

COLOSSAL!

As wide as a chunk of continental coastline and twenty miles high.

PERFECT!

But how will this rock turn into a mountain?

STEP 2:
CRASH AND CRUMPLE

Mountains form when continents collide.

Yes, continents move!

They drift apart, and they crash together.

You may not have noticed, because they move about as fast as your fingernails grow.

When continents collide, rock along the edge can crumple up. Think of your continent like a rug. If you push a rug toward the center, it will crumple into folds. Those are your mountains.

Except this isn't a rug. It's solid rock.
And this is a do-it-yourself project,
so you will be doing the crumpling.

Ready?

Place your hands, brace your feet, and push.

Really PUUUUUUSH!

Put some muscle into it.

Is it crumpling yet?

You may need some help, *lots* of help. This step takes a while—millions of years, in fact. I hope you brought some snacks.

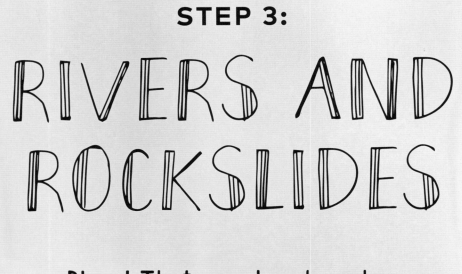

STEP 3:
RIVERS AND ROCKSLIDES

Phew! That was hard work.

You have buckled the edge of your
continent into a fine mountain—
a mountain range, actually.

It's HUGE!

I think it needs a bit more character, though.

Some steep ravines would be nice.

All you'll need for this step is time and weather. The more, the better.

Fortunately, more rain and snow fall on
mountaintops than in valleys below, because
it's cooler above.

As moist air rises to pass over a mountain,
it cools. Cooler air can't hold as much moisture,
so it's released as rain or snow.

Water flowing down your mountain will begin to carve the rock, forming steep gorges. Steeper mountainsides will mean raging rivers and massive landslides.

Time to find cover.

Scan your mountain's slopes.
Did you happen to make any caves?

Many thousands of years later you'll have one rugged mountain! But you aren't done yet.

Your mountain needs some more shaping—
just a little. Let's consider bringing in a glacier.

STEP 4:
FREEZE

Earth has a long history of changing climate patterns.

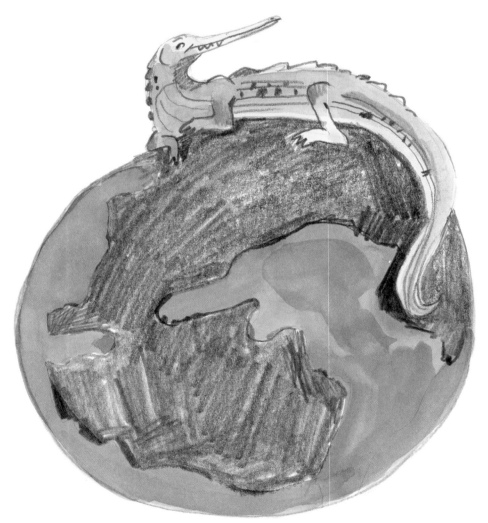

From warm to cool and back again, some changes are small and some huge. Fifty million years ago, Earth was so warm the ancestors of crocodiles lived in the Arctic. Yes! Perhaps you weren't counting on an encounter with a large reptile.

But hang on! Two and a half million years ago, the climate was in a cooling phase.

Glaciers began to form near the north and south poles and in higher elevations, where it is often colder.

A glacier forms when snow piles up over
time. It compresses into a dense sheet of ice
that eventually begins to move slowly, like a
bulldozer, scraping over everything in its path.

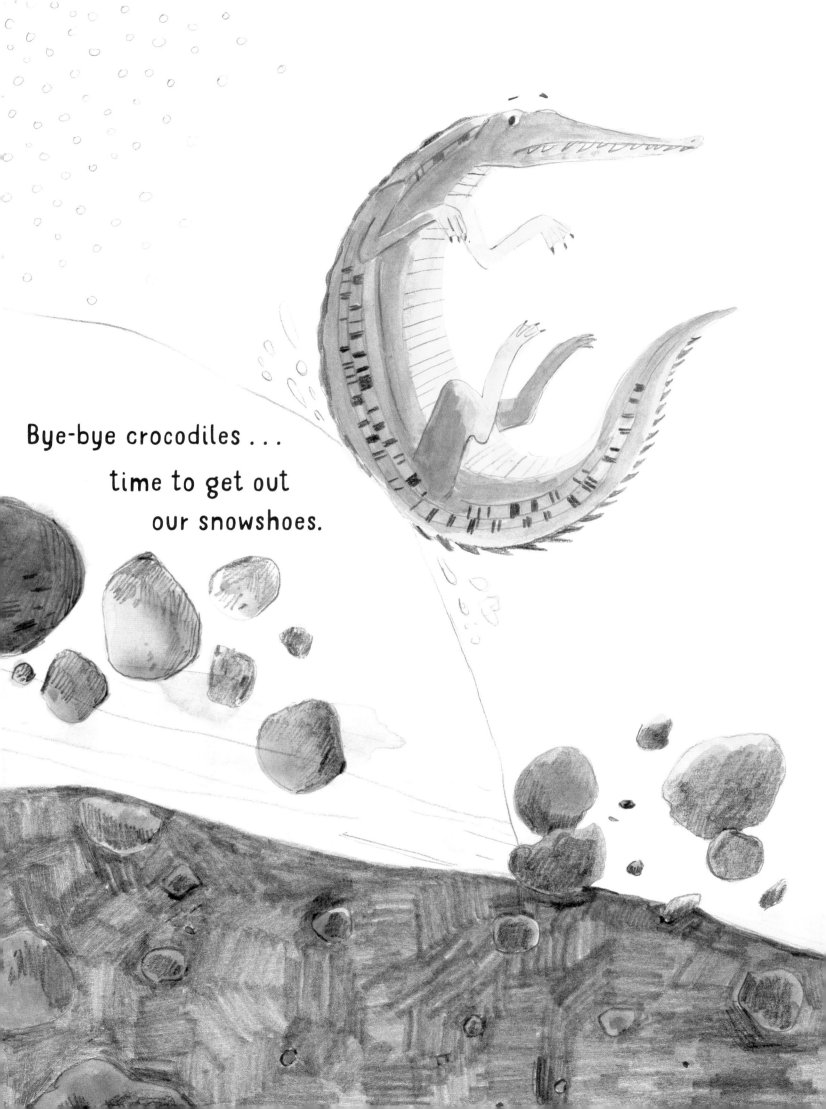

Bye-bye crocodiles . . .
time to get out
our snowshoes.

To make a glacier, you'll need *lots* of snow over a long period of time. Head north.

Gather the coldest weather you can find and snowmaking machines, bazillions of them.

This could take a while. Let's say tens of thousands of years. Put on your warmest mittens, and start practicing your ice-building skills.

It's gonna get chilly!

As it continues to snow,
your glacier will grow and move,
sculpting your mountain and
carving deeper valleys.

The glacier's sheet can be
more than a mile high in places.

CREVASSE

(Look out so you don't
fall into any crevasses!)

Rock sheared off your mountain on one side will be dumped on the other side as the glacier passes.

But you can't see any of that yet.
It's all happening under a thick slab of ice!

. . . Now what?

STEP 5:

MELT

At this point I would think about warming the climate.

Let's see what's under this glacier.
Travel south. Bring fans.

Blow some of that warm southern air
northward to start melting the ice.

Can you feel the temperature change?

Lose the mittens.

Your melting ice will turn into rivers. Gravel, rocks, and giant boulders scraped up over thousands of years will be carried downstream.

They may even block up a valley, creating a lake. Did you bring a kayak?

Ten thousand or so years later and you will finally see your mountain. It's beautiful!

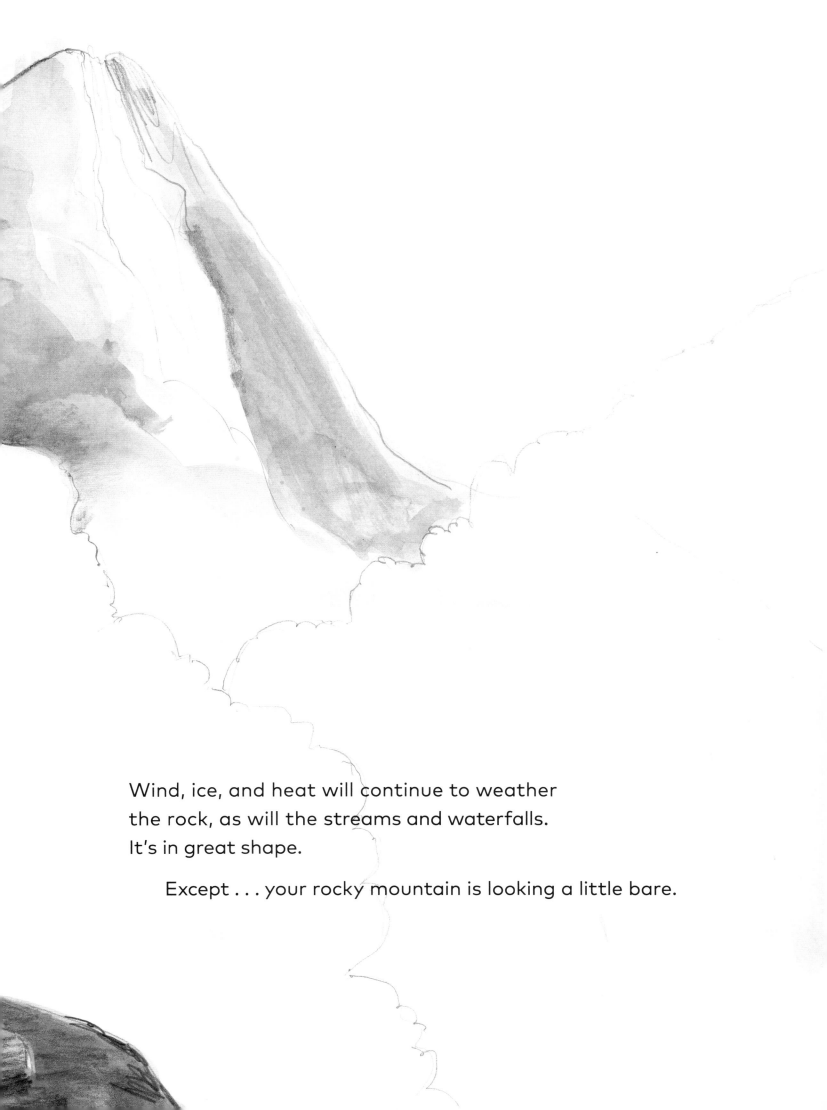

Wind, ice, and heat will continue to weather
the rock, as will the streams and waterfalls.
It's in great shape.

Except . . . your rocky mountain is looking a little bare.

STEP 6:

SOIL

I'm guessing that by now you are itching to add some green to your landscape.

You have a perfect environment for many kinds of plants, except for one minor detail—soil!

As your glaciers melted, they left behind eroded debris of sand, silt, and clay. That's a good start.

Try adding some lichens as well. Lichen looks like a plant, but it's actually a fungus and an alga together.

Place your lichens on the rocks. They will gradually dissolve the rocks, releasing elements that plants can use as nutrients.

It's a *sloooow* process, but while you're waiting,

let's brainstorm a list of plants.

STEP 7:

PLANTS

Lots of different plants
grow on a mountain.

MOSS AND LICHENS

ALPINE MEADOWS

The plants at the bottom will be
different from those at the top.
You'll want some ferns, grasses,
sedges, flowers, shrubs, and
trees, to name a few.

CONIFER FORESTS

MIXED FORESTS

DECIDUOUS FORESTS

Plants on the summit will need to be able to withstand more cold, wind, and ice.

Plants at the bottom will tend to grow larger and faster.

FOREST N[...]

On other mountains, plants' seeds are introduced in several ways.

Sometimes animals who have eaten them nearby poop them out elsewhere in their travels.

A bird might drop a seed in a bit
of soil, where it can sprout.

But for this do-it-yourself project,
you'll be adding the plants.

As your lichens continue to do their work,
wind, ice, and water will also be slowly
breaking down rock into nutrients. You can
begin to introduce mosses and small plants.

As they die and decay, voilà! More soil.

Allow a thousand years or more for this step.

STEP 8:
ANIMALS

What's still missing? Animals!

You *could* let them migrate to your mountain from nearby areas, but this is *your* project.

So add them as you are adding plants, from tiny insects to snakes and salamanders, from frogs, mice, squirrels, raccoons, and skunks to birds, bears, deer, bobcats, and moose.

More plants mean more food and cover for more animals.

You're going to be busy, but eventually your mountain will be teeming with wildlife, and you will finally be nearing the end of your project.

It has been a *looonnnng* project.

You have made and shaped an entire mountain. A variety of healthy plants and animals are thriving there.

Congratulations!
You did it, and it is AMAZING.

One more step to go.

STEP 9:

CARE

Take good care of this mountain.

Generally you'll find that mountains are low-maintenance, but your mountain will still need you to watch over it.

You'll want to keep the streams clean and the bears fed with patches of blueberries and harvests of nuts. Add a few trails so that people can come visit your mountain.

You may want to let other hikers know about the delicate alpine plants at the top and the ravens or bobcats nesting on the ledge.

Are the trees healthy? Are you keeping an eye on the songbirds?

It's a big job, but after all, you just made a mountain!

I think you're up for it.

For right now, let's climb this narrow path,
past the towering cliffs and the waterfall,
right up to the rocky summit.

I love the lake. Nice job on the foothills.

You really went all out!

Ahhhh!

Let's sit here for a while.
Did you bring snacks?

ADDITIONAL

MOUNTAIN-CRAFTING

PROJECTS

Alpine meadow: If you've made a high mountain, an alpine meadow could be perfect! Plants found here would be similar to those growing as your glacier was melting or those you could find today in a tundra or at the top of another high mountain range.

Cirque: Carved by ice at the top of a glacial valley, a cirque looks like half of a huge bowl. Sometimes ice can linger in this scooped-out area far into the summer months. So cool on a hot day!

Erratic: An erratic is a large boulder that may be carried by a glacier great distances before being dumped by the melting ice. Geologists can tell something about the path of the glacier by figuring out where the boulder originated. It would be a stunning addition to the side of your mountain or on a nearby hill or meadow.

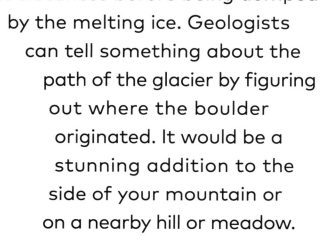

ERRATIC

Hiking trails: If you are planning to open your mountain to hikers, you'll need some trails. You can plan some easy routes and some more difficult climbs. If you set short logs across trails, they'll divert rainwater, provide footing, and preserve vegetation when it's muddy. You've named your mountain, of course, but now you'll need to name its landmarks and paths, as well. Make signs with arrows to show directions, and add distance information. You can give trails descriptive names to clue hikers as to what they may see along the way. For example, the Saddle Trail will take them over the saddle and the Hemlock Trail through a beautiful grove of hemlock trees.

Krummholz: This German word means "crooked wood" or "twisted wood" and describes dwarfed trees you can find circling a mountain peak just below the alpine zone. They might be fir or spruce or even birch. Wind and ice have stunted their growth, making them grow sideways, so these rugged plants have a LOT of funky character.

KRUMMHOLZ

Outcrop: An outcrop is bedrock that has been exposed. Granite makes great bedrock, because it is so durable. Add a granite outcrop partway up your slope for some additional views over the valley below.

Pass, saddle, gap: You were really ambitious, and instead of one mountain, you got two! As you walk along the ridge between the two mountain peaks, the lowest point is called a pass, a saddle, or a gap.

Pond: Ponds can be on mountains. You can make one a few different ways. It could be in a depression made by the glacier, or you could introduce a pair of industrious beavers upslope by one of your babbling brooks.

Striations: Need some texture on some of your exposed rock? Consider striations, striped scratches left as a glacier moves across bedrock. So decorative!

STRIATIONS

VERNAL POOL

Talus: Some cliffs can be broken apart over time by weather and plant roots, creating a slope below of large, chunky rocks. This slope of rock debris is called talus. Add some talus to give your mountain that rugged look.

Vernal pool: At the base of your mountain, think about placing some temporary pools that show up every spring and dry out later in the summer. These are places where numerous frogs, toads, and salamanders can breed every year.

AFTERWORD

The story of Earth and its mountains is complex. Mountains are formed in many ways by many different forces.

The surface of the earth is made up of large plates of rock that hold land and ocean. Over billions of years, these plates have been slowly moving. Large chunks of land have pulled apart and come together, scraping, buckling, folding, and erupting as lava.

By studying the rock in different places all over the world, geologists learn how plates moved and how different mountains were—and still are!—formed by forces deep within the earth. Scientists also study the role glaciers and other kinds of erosion play in reshaping lands and oceans.

And Earth's history continues to unfold. Mountains that we see today would have looked very different millions of years ago. Plants and animals living there would have been different as well.

Earth is always changing. The plates continue to drift! Glaciers carve. Rivers erode mountains, filling valleys with sand, gravel, and stone. One day, millions of years from now, our own familiar mountains will have disappeared and new ones will have risen.

All it will take is a lot of patience, a good push, and a big, big rock.